STEP-BY-STEP

Chinese Szechuan Cooking

Chinese Szechuan Cooking

DEH–TA HSIUNG

||| •PARRAGON• |||

First published in Great Britain in 1994 by
Parragon Book Service Ltd
Unit 13-17, Avonbridge Trading Estate
Atlantic Road
Avonmouth
Bristol BS11 9QD

ISBN 1 85813 639 3

Printed in Italy

Acknowledgements:

Design & DTP: Pedro & Frances Prá-Lopez / Kingfisher Design
Art Direction: Lisa Tai
Managing Editor: Alexa Stace
Special Photography: Amanda Heywood
Home Economist: Deh-ta Hsiung
Stylist: Marian Price

Gas Hob supplied by New World Domestic Appliances Ltd
Food and equipment kindly supplied by Wing Yip
Photographs on pages 6, 18, 28, 40 & 58: By courtesy of ZEFA

Note:
Cup measurements in this book are for American cups. Tablespoons are assumed to be 15ml.

Contents

CHAPTER ONE

Appetizers

Appetizers are often served as starters in Szechuan – just like
hors d'oeuvres in the West. One of the advantages of these
dishes is that they are generally prepared and even cooked
well in advance – hours before serving if need be.
Also almost all the dishes selected here are ideal for
a buffet-style meal or as party food.

Instead of serving different appetizers individually, you can serve a
small portion of each together as an assortment. Select a
minimum of three or four different items:
Deep-fried Prawns (Shrimp), Bang-bang Chicken,
Deep-fried Spare-ribs and so on.

Other dishes that can be served as a part of the appetizer selection
are Szechuan Prawns (Shrimp), Sweet & Sour Prawns (Shrimp),
Aromatic & Crispy Duck, and Braised Chinese Leaves.
Remember not to have more than one of the same type of food,
and the ingredients should be chosen for their
harmony and balance in colour, aroma,
flavour and texture.

Opposite: *The Great Wall
snakes across many miles of
this vast country.*

STEP 1

STEP 2

STEP 3

STEP 4

DEEP-FRIED PRAWNS (SHRIMP)

*For best results, use raw tiger prawns (shrimp) in their shells.
They are 7-10 cm/3-4 in long, and you should get about
18-20 prawns (shrimp) per 500 g/1 lb.*

SERVES 4

*250-300 g/8-10 oz raw prawns (shrimp)
  in their shells, defrosted if frozen
1 tbsp light soy sauce
1 tsp Chinese rice wine or dry sherry
2 tsp cornflour (cornstarch)
vegetable oil, for deep-frying
2-3 spring onions (scallions), to garnish*

SPICY SALT AND PEPPER:
*1 tbsp salt
1 tsp ground Szechuan peppercorns
1 tsp five-spice powder*

1 Pull the soft legs off the prawns (shrimp), and keep the body shell on. Dry well on paper towels.

2 Place the prawns (shrimp) in a bowl with the soy sauce, wine and cornflour (cornstarch). Turn to coat and leave to marinate for about 25-30 minutes.

3 To make the Spicy Salt and Pepper, mix the salt, pepper and five-spice powder together. Place in a dry frying pan and stir-fry for about 3-4 minutes over a low heat, stirring constantly. Remove from the heat and allow to cool.

4 Heat the oil in a preheated wok until smoking, then deep-fry the prawns (shrimp) in batches until golden brown. Remove with a slotted spoon and drain on paper towels.

5 Place the spring onions (scallions) in a bowl, pour on 1 tablespoon of the hot oil, and leave for 30 seconds. Serve the prawns (shrimp) garnished with the spring onions (scallions), and with Spicy Salt and Pepper as a dip.

ROASTING SPICES

The roasted spice mixture made with Szechuan peppercorns is used throughout China as a dip for deep-fried food. The peppercorns are sometimes roasted first and then ground. Dry-frying is a way of releasing the flavours of the spices. You can make the dip in advance and store in a tightly sealed jar until ready to use.

STEP 1

STEP 2

STEP 3

STEP 4

PORK WITH CHILLI & GARLIC

Any leftovers from this dish can be used for a number of other dishes –
such as Hot & Sour Soup (page 20), and Twice-cooked Pork (page 53).

SERVES 4

500 g/ 1 lb leg of pork, boned but not
  skinned

SAUCE:
1 tsp finely chopped garlic
1 tsp finely chopped spring onions
  (scallions)
2 tbsp light soy sauce
1 tsp red chilli oil
$^1/_2$ tsp sesame oil

1 Place the pork, tied together in one
piece, in a large pan, add enough
cold water to cover, and bring to a rolling
boil over a medium heat.

2 Skim off the scum that rises to the
surface, cover and simmer gently
for 25-30 minutes.

3 Leave the meat in the liquid to cool,
under cover, for at least 1-2 hours.
Lift out the meat with 2 slotted spoons
and leave to cool completely, skin-side
up, for 2-3 hours.

4 To serve, cut off the skin, leaving a
very thin layer of fat on top like a
ham joint. Cut the meat in small thin
slices across the grain, and arrange

neatly on a plate. Mix together the sauce
ingredients, and pour the sauce evenly
over the pork.

SZECHUAN CHILLI

One of the local Szechuan plants that
contributes most to the typical character of
the region's cooking is the small red
fagara chilli, which is used both fresh and
dried. The chilli has a delayed action on
the palate; at first it seems to have little
taste, but suddenly it burns the mouth
with great ferocity, so it is used with much
respect. It is claimed that instead of
burning the taste-buds, the chilli actually
makes them more sensitive to other
flavours.

This is a very simple dish, but
beautifully presented. Make sure you slice
the meat as thinly and evenly as possible
to make an elegantly arranged dish.

BANG-BANG CHICKEN

The cooked chicken meat is tenderized by being beaten with a rolling pin, hence the name for this very popular Szechuan dish.

STEP 1

SERVES 4

1 litre/1 ³/₄ pints/4 cups water
2 chicken quarters (breast half and leg)
1 cucumber, cut into matchstick shreds

SAUCE:
2 tbsp light soy sauce
1 tsp sugar
1 tbsp finely chopped spring onions
   (scallions)
1 tsp red chilli oil
¹/₄ tsp pepper
1 tsp white sesame seeds
2 tbsp peanut butter, creamed with a little
   sesame oil

1 Bring the water to a rolling boil in a wok or a large pan. Add the chicken pieces, reduce the heat, cover and cook for 30-35 minutes.

2 Remove the chicken from the pan and immerse it in a bowl of cold water for at least 1 hour to cool it, ready for shredding.

3 Remove the chicken pieces and drain well. Dry the chicken pieces on absorbent kitchen paper (paper towels), then take the meat off the bone.

4 On a flat surface, pound the chicken with a rolling pin, then tear the meat into shreds with 2 forks. Mix with the shredded cucumber and arrange in a serving dish.

5 To serve, mix together all the sauce ingredients and pour over the chicken and cucumber.

STEP 2

STEP 4a

THE CHOICEST CHICKEN

This dish is also known as Bon-bon Chicken – bon is a Chinese work for stick, so again the tenderizing technique inspires the recipe name.

Take the time to tear the chicken meat into similar-sized shreds, to make an elegant-looking dish. You can do this quite efficiently with 2 forks, although Chinese cooks would do it with their fingers.

STEP 4b

STEP 1a

STEP 1b

STEP 2

STEP 3

PICKLED CUCUMBER

The pickling takes minutes rather than days – but the longer you leave it, the better the result. Some pickled vegetables are marinated for days – see the recipe for Mixed Pickled Vegetables, below.

SERVES 4

1 slender cucumber, about 30 cm / 12 in long
1 tsp salt
2 tsp caster sugar
1 tsp rice vinegar
1 tsp red chilli oil
a few drops sesame oil

1 Halve the cucumber, unpeeled, lengthways. Scrape off the seeds and cut across into thick chunks.

2 Sprinkle with the salt and mix well. Leave to marinate for at least 20-30 minutes, longer if possible, then pour the juice away.

3 Mix the cucumber with the sugar, vinegar and chilli oil, and sprinkle with the sesame oil just before serving.

MIXED PICKLED VEGETABLES

350 g / 12 oz Chinese leaves, cut into bite-sized pieces
50 g / 2 oz French beans, topped and tailed
125 g / 4 oz carrots, diced
3 chillis, seeded and chopped finely
2 tsp Szechuan peppercorns
2 tbsp coarse salt
2 tbsp rice wine

Place the vegetables in a glass bowl with the chillies, peppercorns, salt and wine. Stir well, cover and leave to marinate in the refrigerator for 4 days. Serve cold, as a salad.

PICKLED VEGETABLES

Pickled vegetables and fruits are very popular with the Chinese. They are often served as snacks and appetizers, and can also be served with cold meat dishes. Usually, the vegetables are allowed to stay in the marinade for 3-4 days. Once made, they will keep in the refrigerator for up to 2 weeks.

STEP 1

STEP 2

STEP 3

STEP 4

DEEP-FRIED SPARE RIBS

*The spare ribs should be chopped into small bite-sized pieces
before or after cooking.*

SERVES 4

*8-10 finger spare ribs
1 tsp five-spice powder or 1 tbsp mild curry
    powder
1 tbsp rice wine or dry sherry
1 egg
2 tbsp flour
vegetable oil, for deep-frying
1 tsp finely shredded spring onions
    (scallions)
1 tsp finely shredded fresh green or red hot
    chillies, seeded
salt and pepper
Spicy Salt and Pepper (see page 8), to serve*

1 Chop the ribs into 3-4 small pieces.
Place the ribs in a bowl with salt,
pepper, five-spice or curry powder and
the wine. Turn to coat the ribs in the
spices and leave them to marinate for
1-2 hours.

2 Mix the egg and flour together to
make a batter.

3 Dip the ribs in the batter one by one
to coat well.

4 Heat the oil in a preheated wok
until smoking. Deep-fry the ribs for
4-5 minutes, then remove with a slotted
spoon and drain on paper towels.

5 Reheat the oil over a high heat and
deep-fry the ribs once more for
another minute. Remove and drain
again on paper towels.

6 Pour 1 tablespoon of the hot oil
over the spring onions (scallions)
and chillies and leave for 30-40 seconds.
Serve the ribs with Spicy Salt and Pepper,
garnished with the shredded spring
onions (scallions) and chillies.

FINGER RIBS

To make finger ribs, cut the sheet of spare
ribs into individual ribs down each side of
the bones. These ribs are then chopped
into bite-sized pieces for deep-frying.

16

CHAPTER TWO

Soups

Soup is not normally served as a separate course in China, except at formal occasions and banquets, when it usually appears towards the end of the meal.

Otherwise, in Chinese homes a simply made soup is served with all the other dishes throughout the meal. The soup is almost always a clear broth in which some thinly sliced vegetables and/or meat have been poached quickly.

The soup should ideally be made with a good stock. If you use a stock cube, remember to reduce the amount of seasoning in the recipes, since most commercially made bouillon cubes are fairly salty and spicy. It is always worth while making your own Chinese stock, following the recipe on page 76, if you have the time.

Opposite: Fresh vegetables on display in a market in Szechuan. The Chinese shop daily in the markets to ensure that produce is absolutely fresh and crisp.

STEP 1

STEP 2

STEP 3

STEP 4

HOT & SOUR SOUP

This is the favourite soup in Chinese restaurants throughout the world.

SERVES 4

*4-6 dried Chinese mushrooms (Shiitake),
  soaked
125 g/4 oz cooked pork or chicken
1 cake tofu (bean curd)
60 g/2 oz canned sliced bamboo shoots,
  drained
600 ml/1 pint/2½ cups Chinese Stock
  (see page 76) or water
1 tbsp Chinese rice wine or dry sherry
1 tbsp light soy sauce
2 tbsp rice vinegar
1 tbsp cornflour (cornstarch) paste
  (see page 77)
salt, to taste
½ tsp ground white pepper
2-3 spring onions (scallions), thinly sliced,
  to serve*

1 Drain the mushrooms, squeeze dry and discard the hard stalks. Thinly slice the mushrooms.

2 Thinly slice the meat, tofu and bamboo shoots into narrow shreds.

3 Bring the stock or water to a rolling boil in a wok or large pan and add all the ingredients. Bring back to the boil then simmer for about 1 minute. Add the wine, soy sauce and vinegar.

4 Bring back to the boil once more, stirring in the cornflour (cornstarch) paste to thicken the soup. Serve hot, sprinkled with the spring onions (scallions).

DRIED MUSHROOMS

There are many varieties of dried mushrooms, which add a particular flavour to Chinese cooking. Shiitake mushrooms are one of the favourite kinds to use. Soak in hot water for 25-30 minutes before use and cut off the hard stems.

  If you strain the soaking liquid through fine cheesecloth, you can use the liquid to give a mushroom flavour to other soups, as well as sauces and casseroles. It is important to strain the liquid carefully because it will contain small, gritty particles.

STEP 1a

STEP 1b

STEP 2

STEP 3

THREE-FLAVOUR SOUP

*Ideally, use raw prawns (shrimp) in this soup. If that is not possible,
add ready-cooked ones at the very last stage.*

SERVES 4

125 g/4 oz skinned, boned chicken breast
125 g/4 oz raw peeled prawns (shrimp)
salt
½ egg white, lightly beaten
2 tsp cornflour (cornstarch) paste
    (see page 77)
125 g/4 oz honey-roast ham
750 ml/1¼ pints/3 cups Chinese Stock
    (see page 76) or water
finely chopped spring onions (scallions), to
    garnish

1 Thinly slice the chicken into small
shreds. If the prawns (shrimp) are
large, cut each in half lengthways,
otherwise leave whole. Place the chicken
and prawns (shrimps) in a bowl and
mix with a pinch of salt, the egg white
and cornflour (cornstarch) paste until
well coated.

2 Cut the ham into small thin slices
roughly the same size as the
chicken pieces.

3 Bring the stock or water to a
rolling boil, add the chicken, the
raw prawns (shrimps) and the ham.
Bring the soup back to the boil, and
simmer for 1 minute.

4 Adjust the seasoning and serve the
soup hot, garnished with the spring
onions (scallions).

COOKING TIPS

Soups such as this are improved
enormously in flavour if you use a well-
flavoured stock. Either use a stock cube, or
find time to make Chinese Stock – see the
recipe on page 76. Better still, make
double quantities and freeze some for
future use.

Fresh, uncooked prawns (shrimp)
impart the best flavour. If these are not
available, you can use ready-cooked
prawns (shrimp). They must be added at
the last moment before serving to prevent
them becoming tough and over-cooked.

STEP 1

STEP 2

STEP 3

STEP 4

PORK & SZECHUAN VEGETABLE

Sold in cans, Szechuan preserved vegetable is pickled mustard root which is quite hot and salty, so rinse in water before use.

SERVES 4

250 g/8 oz pork fillet
2 tsp cornflour (cornstarch) paste
   (see page 77)
125 g/4 oz Szechuan preserved vegetable
750 ml/1¼ pints/3 cups Chinese stock
   (see page 76) or water
salt and pepper
a few drops of sesame oil (optional)
2-3 spring onions (scallions), sliced, to
   garnish

1 Cut the pork across the grain into thin shreds and mix with the cornflour (cornstarch) paste.

2 Wash and rinse the Szechuan preserved vegetable, then cut into thin shreds the same size as the pork.

3 Bring the stock or water to a rolling boil, add the pork and stir to separate the shreds. Return to the boil.

4 Add the Szechuan preserved vegetable and bring back to the boil once more. Adjust the seasoning and sprinkle with sesame oil. Serve hot, garnished with spring onions (scallions).

SZECHUAN PRESERVED VEGETABLE

The Chinese are fond of pickles, and there are many varieties of pickled vegetables. In the Szechuan region in particular, preserved vegetables are important because the region is over 1,600 km (1,000 miles) from the coast. Vinegar and salt (from the province's extensive salt mines) are used to make a range of pickled foods, which are used in cooking and eaten on their own.

One of the most popular is Szechuan preserved vegetable, a speciality of the province, available in cans from specialist Chinese supermarkets. It is actually mustard green root, pickled in salt and chillies. It gives a crunchy, spicy taste to dishes. Rinse in cold water before use. Once opened the vegetable should be stored in a tightly sealed jar and kept in the refrigerator.

SPINACH & TOFU SOUP

*This is a very colourful and delicious soup. If spinach is not in season,
watercress or lettuce can be used instead.*

STEP 1a

SERVES 4

1 cake tofu (bean curd)
125 g/4 oz spinach leaves without stems
750 ml/1¼ pints/3 cups Chinese Stock
   (see page 76) or water
1 tbsp light soy sauce
salt and pepper

STEP 1b

1 Cut the tofu into small pieces about 5 mm (¼ in) thick. Wash the spinach leaves and cut them into small pieces or shreds, discarding any discoloured leaves and tough stalks. (If possible, use fresh young spinach leaves, which have not yet developed tough ribs. Otherwise, it is important to cut out all the ribs and stems for this soup.)

2 In a wok or large pan, bring the stock to a rolling boil, add the tofu and soy sauce, bring back to the boil and simmer for about 2 minutes over a medium heat.

3 Add the spinach and simmer for 1 more minute.

4 Skim the surface of the soup to make it clear, adjust the seasoning and serve.

STEP 2

> ## SERVING SUGGESTIONS
>
> There is no set order of courses for Chinese meals. The soup is an integral part of the meal; it may be served first, but people can help themselves to more during the meal. The soup is usually presented in a large bowl placed in the centre of the table, and consumed as the meal progresses. It serves as a refresher between different dishes and as a beverage throughout the meal. (Water is never served during the meal, and tea is brought only before and after a meal.)
>
> Each person at the table has a bowl, rather than a plate, that is used for all dishes. Chopsticks are used for picking up the food – or in the case of soups, a broad, shallow spoon.

STEP 3

CHAPTER THREE

Seafood Dishes

As in the rest of China, Szechuan food features fish in many dishes, especially freshwater fish from the mighty Yangtse river, which flows through the region.

Szechuan dishes are noted for their hot, spicy character, and fish and seafood dishes are no exception. Whole fish, and fish fillets, are served in thick, spicy sauces, as in Braised Fish Fillets (page 37). Prawn dishes are equally hot and spicy, with garlic, ginger and chilli appearing in almost every recipe – Szechuan Prawn (Shrimp) (see page 33) is a typical example.

Opposite: The Yangtse River near Guilin. Until recently the Yangtse was Szechuan's main avenue of communication with the rest of China.

SWEET & SOUR PRAWNS (SHRIMP)

Use raw prawns (shrimp) if possible. Omit steps 1 and 2 if ready-cooked ones are used.

STEP 2

STEP 3a

STEP 3b

STEP 4

SERVES 4

175-250 g/6-8 oz peeled raw tiger prawns
pinch of salt
1 tsp egg white
1 tsp cornflour (cornstarch) paste (see page 77)
300 ml/¹/₂ pint/ 1¹/₄ cups vegetable oil

SAUCE:
1 tbsp vegetable oil
¹/₂ small green (bell) pepper, cored, seeded and thinly sliced
¹/₂ small carrot, thinly sliced
125 g/4 oz canned water chestnuts, drained and sliced
¹/₂ tsp salt
1 tbsp light soy sauce
2 tbsp sugar
3 tbsp rice or sherry vinegar
1 tsp rice wine or dry sherry
1 tbsp tomato sauce
¹/₂ tsp chilli sauce
3-4 tbsp Chinese Stock (see page 76) or water
2 tsp cornflour (cornstarch) paste (see page 77)
a few drops of sesame oil

1 Mix the prawns (shrimp) with the salt, egg white and cornflour (cornstarch) paste.

2 Heat the oil in a preheated wok and stir-fry the prawns (shrimp) for 30-40 seconds only. Remove and drain on paper towels.

3 Pour off the oil and wipe the wok clean with paper towels. To make the sauce, first heat the tablespoon of oil. Add the vegetables and stir-fry for about 1 minute, then add the seasonings with the stock or water and bring to the boil.

4 Add the prawns (shrimp) and stir until blended well. Thicken the sauce with the cornflour (cornstarch) paste and stir until smooth. Sprinkle with sesame oil and serve hot.

SESAME OIL

Sesame oil has a distinctive nutty flavour and aroma. It is widely used in China as a seasoning and is usually sprinkled on at the last moment, to finish a dish. It is now widely available. Use sparingly.

SZECHUAN PRAWNS (SHRIMP)

Raw prawns (shrimp) should be used if possible, otherwise omit steps 1 and 2 and add the ready-cooked prawns (shrimp) before the sauce ingredients at the beginning of step 3.

STEP 1

SERVES 4

250-300 g/8-10 oz raw tiger prawns (shrimp)
pinch of salt
½ egg white, lightly beaten
1 tsp cornflour (cornstarch) paste (see page 77)
600 ml/1pint/2½ cups vegetable oil
fresh coriander leaves, to garnish

SAUCE:

1 tsp finely chopped ginger root
2 spring onions (scallions), finely chopped
1 garlic clove, finely chopped
3-4 small dried red chillies, seeded and chopped
1 tbsp light soy sauce
1 tsp rice wine or dry sherry
1 tbsp tomato purée (paste)
1 tbsp oyster sauce
2-3 tbsp Chinese Stock (see page 76) or water
a few drops of sesame oil

1 Peel the raw prawns (shrimp), then mix with the salt, egg white and cornflour (cornstarch) paste until well coated.

2 Heat the oil in a preheated wok until it is smoking, then deep-fry the prawns (shrimp) in hot oil for about 1 minute. Remove with a slotted spoon and drain on paper towels.

3 Pour off the oil, leaving about 1 tablespoon in the wok. Add all the ingredients for the sauce, bring to the boil and stir until smooth and well blended.

4 Add the prawns (shrimp) to the sauce and stir until blended well. Serve garnished with coriander leaves.

STEP 2

STEP 3

CHILLIES

In Szechuan dishes chillies are often left unseeded, giving an extremely hot flavour to dishes. If you dislike very hot food, make sure the dried chillies are carefully seeded before use.

STEP 4

STEP 1

STEP 2

STEP 3

STEP 4

STIR-FRIED PRAWNS (SHRIMP)

The (bell) peppers in this dish can be replaced by either mangetout (snow peas), or broccoli – the idea is to contrast the pinky/orange prawns (shrimp) with a bright green vegetable.

SERVES 4

170 g/6 oz raw prawns (shrimp), peeled
1 tsp salt
$1/4$ tsp egg white
2 tsp cornflour (cornstarch) paste (see page 77)
300 ml/$1/2$ pint/$1 1/4$ cups vegetable oil
1 spring onion (scallion), cut into short sections
2.5 cm (1 in) ginger root, thinly sliced
1 small green (bell) pepper, cored, seeded and cubed
$1/2$ tsp sugar
1 tbsp light soy sauce
1 tsp rice wine or dry sherry
a few drops of sesame oil

1 Mix the prawns (shrimp) with a pinch of the salt, the egg white and cornflour (cornstarch) paste until they are all well coated.

2 Heat the oil in a preheated wok and stir-fry the prawns (shrimp) for 30-40 seconds only. Remove and drain on paper towels.

3 Pour off the oil, leaving about 1 tablespoon in the wok. Add the spring onion (scallion) and ginger to flavour the oil for a few seconds, then add the green (bell) pepper and stir-fry for about 1 minute.

4 Add the remaining salt and the sugar followed by the prawns (shrimp). Continue stirring for another minute or so, then add the soy sauce and wine and blend well. Sprinkle with sesame oil and serve immediately.

COOK'S HINTS

1-2 small green or red hot chillies, sliced, can be added with the green (bell) pepper to create a more spicy dish. Leave the chillies unseeded for a very hot dish.

Fresh ginger root, sold by weight, should be peeled and sliced, then finely chopped or shredded before use. It will keep for weeks in a cool, dry place. Dried ginger powder is no substitute – in comparison with fresh ginger root, it is lacking in flavour.

BRAISED FISH FILLETS

Any white fish such as lemon sole or plaice is ideal for this dish.

STEP 2

SERVES 4

3-4 small Chinese dried mushrooms
300-350 g/10-12 oz fish fillets
1 tsp salt
$^1\!/_2$ egg white, lightly beaten
1 tsp cornflour (cornstarch) paste (see
 page 77)
600 ml/1 pint/2$^1\!/_2$ cups vegetable oil
1 tsp finely chopped ginger root
2 spring onions (scallions), finely chopped
1 garlic clove, finely chopped
$^1\!/_2$ small green (bell) pepper, cored, seeded
 and cut into small cubes
$^1\!/_2$ small carrot, thinly sliced
60 g/2 oz canned sliced bamboo shoots,
 rinsed and drained
$^1\!/_2$ tsp sugar
1 tbsp light soy sauce
1 tsp rice wine or dry sherry
1 tbsp chilli bean sauce
2-3 tbsp Chinese Stock (see page 76) or
 water
a few drops of sesame oil

1 Soak the Chinese mushrooms in warm water for 30 minutes, then drain on paper towels, reserving the soaking water for stock or soup. Squeeze the mushrooms to extract all the moisture, cut off and discard any hard stems and slice thinly.

2 Cut the fish into bite-sized pieces, then place in a shallow dish and mix with a pinch of salt, the egg white and cornflour (cornstarch) paste, turning the fish to coat well.

3 Heat the oil and deep-fry the fish pieces for about 1 minute. Remove with a slotted spoon and drain on paper towels.

4 Pour off the oil, leaving about 1 tablespoon in the wok. Add the ginger, spring onions (scallions) and garlic to flavour the oil for a few seconds, then add the vegetables and stir-fry for about 1 minute.

5 Add the salt, sugar, soy sauce, wine, chilli bean sauce and stock or water and bring to the boil. Add the fish pieces, stir to coat well with the sauce, and braise for another minute. Sprinkle with sesame oil and serve immediately.

STEP 3

STEP 4

STEP 5

STEP 1

STEP 2

STEP 3a

STEP 3b

FISH IN SZECHUAN HOT SAUCE

This is a classic Szechuan recipe. When served in a restaurant, the fish head and tail are removed before cooking.

SERVES 4

1 carp, bream, sea bass, trout, grouper or
    grey mullet, about 750g/1½ lb, gutted
1 tbsp light soy sauce
1 tbsp Chinese rice wine or dry sherry
vegetable oil, for deep-frying
flat-leaf parsley or coriander sprigs, to
    garnish

SAUCE:
2 garlic cloves, finely chopped
2-3 spring onions (scallions), finely chopped
1 tsp finely chopped ginger root
2 tbsp chilli bean sauce
1 tbsp tomato purée (paste)
2 tsp sugar
1 tbsp rice vingar
125 ml/4 fl oz/½ cup Chinese Stock(see
    page 76) or water
1 tbsp cornflour (cornstarch) paste (see
    page 77)
½ tsp sesame oil

1 Wash the fish and dry well on paper towels. Score both sides of the fish to the bone with a sharp knife, making diagonal cuts at intervals of about 2.5 cm/1 in. Rub the fish with the soy sauce and wine on both sides, then leave on a plate in the refrigerator to marinate for 10-15 minutes.

2 Heat the oil in a preheated wok until smoking. Deep-fry the fish in the hot oil for about 3-4 minutes on both sides, or until golden brown.

3 Pour off the oil, leaving about 1 tablespoon in the wok. Push the fish to one side of the wok and add the garlic, white parts of the spring onions (scallions), ginger, chilli bean sauce, tomato purée (paste), sugar, vinegar and stock. Bring to the boil and braise the fish in the sauce for 4-5 minutes, turning it over once.

4 Add the green parts of the spring onions (scallions) and stir in the cornflour (cornstarch) paste to thicken the sauce. Sprinkle with sesame oil and serve immediately, garnished with parsley or coriander.

CHAPTER FOUR

Meat & Poultry Dishes

Poultry is popular in Szechuan as elsewhere in China, though characteristically it is much hotter and spicier than elsewhere – Chilli Chicken (page 47) is a typical example.

Beef appears on the menu more often than in the South or East. A favourite form of cooking is stir-frying, giving a dry, chewy texture. Braising and steaming are also popular methods of cooking beef and pork, ensuring a tender result, and so too is double-cooking. This is a technique in which the meat is first tenderized by long, slow simmering in water, followed by a quick crisping or stir-frying in a sauce – Twice-cooked Pork (page 53) is a delicious example of this technique.

Opposite: *The fertile soil of Szechuan produces abundant crops almost all the year round.*

STEP 1

STEP 2a

STEP 2b

STEP 4

AROMATIC & CRISPY DUCK

Although the pancakes traditionally served with this dish are not too difficult to make, the process is very time-consuming. Buy ready-made ones from Oriental stores, or use crisp lettuce leaves as the wrapper.

SERVES 4

2 large duckling quarters
1 tsp salt
3-4 pieces star anise
1 tsp Szechuan red peppercorns
1 tsp cloves
2 cinnamon sticks, broken into pieces
2-3 spring onions (scallions), cut into short sections
4-5 small slices ginger root
3-4 tbsp rice wine or dry sherry
vegetable oil, for deep-frying

TO SERVE:
12 ready-made pancakes or 12 crisp lettuce leaves
hoi-sin or plum sauce
1/4 cucumber, thinly shredded
3-4 spring onions (scallions), thinly shredded

1 Rub the duck pieces with the salt and arrange the star anise, peppercorns, cloves and cinnamon on top. Sprinkle with the spring onions (scallions), ginger and wine and leave to marinate for at least 3-4 hours.

2 Arrange the duck pieces (with the marinade spices) on a plate that will fit inside a bamboo steamer. Pour some hot water into a wok, place the bamboo steamer in the wok, sitting on a trivet. Put in the duck and cover with the bamboo lid. Steam the duck pieces (with the marinade) over high heat for at least 2-3 hours, until tender and cooked through. Top up the hot water from time to time as required.

3 Remove the duck and leave to cool for at least 4-5 hours – this is very important, for unless the duck is cold and dry, it will not be crispy.

4 Pour off the water and wipe the wok dry. Pour in the oil and heat until smoking. Deep-fry the duck pieces, skin-side down, for 4-5 minutes or until crisp and brown. Remove and drain on paper towels.

5 To serve, scrape the meat off the bone, place about 1 teaspoon of hoi-sin or plum sauce on the centre of a pancake (or lettuce leaf), add a few pieces of cucumber and spring onion (scallion) with a portion of the duck meat. Wrap up to form a small parcel and eat with your fingers. Provide plenty of paper napkins for your guests.

42

STEP 1

STEP 2

STEP 3

STEP 4

KUNG PO CHICKEN WITH CASHEW

Peanuts, walnuts or almonds can be used instead of the cashew nuts, if preferred.

SERVES 4

*250-300 g/8-10 oz chicken meat, boned
 and skinned*
¼ tsp salt
⅓ egg white
*1 tsp cornflour (cornstarch) paste (see
 page 77)*
*1 medium green (bell) pepper, cored and
 seeded*
4 tbsp vegetable oil
*1 spring onion (scallion), cut into short
 sections*
a few small slices of ginger root
*4-5 small dried red chillies, soaked, seeded
 and shredded*
2 tbsp crushed yellow bean sauce
1 tsp rice wine or dry sherry
125 g/4 oz roasted cashew nuts
a few drops of sesame oil
boiled rice, to serve

1 Cut the chicken into small cubes
about the size of sugar lumps.
Place the chicken in a small bowl and
mix with a pinch of salt, the egg white
and the cornflour (cornstarch) paste, in
that order.

2 Cut the green (bell) pepper into
cubes or triangles about the same
size as the chicken pieces.

3 Heat the oil in a preheated wok,
add the chicken cubes and stir-fry
for about 1 minute, or until the colour
changes. Remove with a slotted spoon
and keep warm.

4 Add the spring onion (scallion),
ginger, chillies and green (bell)
pepper. Stir-fry for about 1 minute, then
add the chicken with the yellow bean
sauce and wine. Blend well and stir-fry
for another minute. Finally stir in the
cashew nuts and sesame oil. Serve hot.

VARIATIONS

Any nuts can be used in place of the
cashew nuts, if preferred. The important
point is the crunchy texture, which is very
much a feature of Szechuan cooking.

SZECHUAN CHILLI CHICKEN

In China, the chicken pieces are chopped through the bone for this dish, but if you do not possess a cleaver, use filleted chicken meat.

STEP 1

SERVES 4

500 g/1 lb chicken thighs
¼ tsp pepper
1 tbsp sugar
2 tsp light soy sauce
1 tsp dark soy sauce
1 tbsp rice wine or dry sherry
2 tsp cornflour (cornstarch)
2-3 tbsp vegetable oil
1-2 garlic cloves, crushed
2 spring onions (scallions), cut into short
*   sections, with the green and white parts*
*   separated*
4-6 small dried red chillies, soaked and
*   seeded*
2 tbsp crushed yellow bean sauce
about 150 ml/¼ pint/⅔ cup Chinese Stock
*   (see page 76) or water*

1 Cut or chop the chicken thighs into bite-sized pieces and marinate with the pepper, sugar, soy sauce, wine and cornflour (cornstarch) for 25-30 minutes.

2 Heat the oil in a pre-heated wok, add the chicken pieces and stir-fry until lightly brown for about 1-2 minutes. Remove the chicken pieces with a slotted spoon, remove to a warm dish and reserve.

3 Add the garlic, the white parts of the spring onions (scallions), the chillies and yellow bean sauce to the wok and stir-fry for about 30 seconds, blending well.

4 Return the chicken pieces to the wok, stirring constantly for about 1-2 minutes, then add the stock or water, bring to the boil and cover. Braise over medium heat for 5-6 minutes, stirring once or twice. Garnish with the green parts of the spring onions (scallions) and serve immediately.

STEP 2

STEP 3

CHILLIES

One of the striking features of Szechuan cooking is the quantity of chillies used. Food generally in this region is much hotter than elsewhere in China – people tend to keep a string of dry chillies hanging from the eaves of their houses.

STEP 4

47

STEP 1

STEP 2

STEP 3

STEP 4

CHICKEN WITH (BELL) PEPPERS

Red (bell) pepper or celery can also be used in recipe,
the method is the same.

SERVES 4

300 g/10 oz boned, skinned chicken breast
1 tsp salt
½ egg white
2 tsp cornflour (cornstarch) paste (see
page 77)
1 medium green (bell) pepper, cored and
seeded
300 ml/½ pint/1¼ cups vegetable oil
1 spring onion (scallion), finely shredded
a few strips of ginger root, thinly shredded
1-2 red chillies, seeded and thinly shredded
½ tsp sugar
1 tbsp rice wine or dry sherry
a few drops of sesame oil

1 Cut the chicken breast into strips,
then mix in a bowl with a pinch of
the salt, the egg white and cornflour
(cornstarch), in that order.

2 Cut the green (bell) pepper into
thin shreds the same size and
length as the chicken strips.

3 Heat the oil in a preheated wok,
and deep-fry the chicken strips in
batches for about 1 minute, or until the
colour of the chicken changes. Remove
the chicken strips with a slotted spoon
and keep warm.

4 Pour off the excess oil from the
wok, leaving about 1 tablespoon.
Add the spring onion (scallion), ginger,
chillies and green (bell) pepper. Stir-fry
for about 1 minute, then return the
chicken to the wok together with the
remaining salt, the sugar and wine. Stir-
fry for another minute, sprinkle with
sesame oil and serve.

RICE WINE

Rice wine is used everywhere in China for
both cooking and drinking. Made from
glutinous rice, it is known as "yellow
wine" (Huang jiu or chiew in Chinese)
because of its rich amber colour. The best
variety is called Shao Hsing or Shaoxing,
and comes from the south-east of China.
Rice wine is more powerful than wines in
the West – about 16° proof – and sherry is
the best substitute as a cooking
ingredient.

STEP 1a

STEP 1b

STEP 3

STEP 4

FISH-FLAVOURED SHREDDED PORK

*"Fish-flavoured" (yu-xiang in Chinese) is a Szechuan cookery term
meaning that the dish is prepared with seasonings
normally used in fish dishes.*

SERVES 4

about 2 tbsp dried wood ears
250-300 g/8-10 oz pork fillet
1 tsp salt
*2 tsp cornflour (cornstarch) paste (see
   page 77)*
3 tbsp vegetable oil
1 garlic clove, finely chopped
1/2 tsp finely chopped ginger root
*2 spring onions (scallions), finely chopped,
   with the white and green parts separated*
2 celery stalks, thinly sliced
1/2 tsp sugar
1 tbsp light soy sauce
1 tbsp chilli bean sauce
2 tsp rice vinegar
1 tsp rice wine or dry sherry
a few drops of sesame oil

1 Soak the wood ears in warm water
for about 20 minutes, then rinse in
cold water until the water is clear. Drain
well, then cut into thin shreds.

2 Cut the pork into thin shreds, then
mix in a bowl with a pinch of salt
and about half the cornflour (cornstarch)
paste until well coated.

3 Heat 1 tablespoon of oil in a
preheated wok. Add the pork strips

and stir-fry for about 1 minute, or until
the colour changes, then remove with a
slotted spoon.

4 Add the remaining oil to the wok
and heat. Add the garlic, ginger,
the white parts of the spring onions
(scallions), the wood ears and celery.
Stir-fry for about 1 minute, then return
the pork strips together with the salt,
sugar, soy sauce, chili bean sauce,
vinegar and wine. Blend well and
continue stirring for another minute.

5 Finally add the green parts of the
spring onions (scallions) and blend
in the remaining cornflour (cornstarch)
paste and sesame oil. Stir until the sauce
has thickened and serve hot.

DRIED WOOD EARS

Also known as cloud ears, this is a dried
grey-black fungus widely used in
Szechuan cooking. It is always soaked in
warm water before using. Wood ears have
a crunchy texture and a mild flavour.

TWICE-COOKED PORK

Twice-cooked is a popular way of cooking meat in China. The meat is first boiled to tenderize it, then cut into strips or slices and stir-fried.

STEP 1a

STEP 1b

STEP 2

STEP 4

SERVES 4

250-300 g/8-10 oz shoulder or leg of pork,
   in one piece
1 small green (bell) pepper, cored and seeded
1 small red (bell) pepper, cored and seeded
125 g/4 oz canned sliced bamboo shoots,
   rinsed and drained
3 tbsp vegetable oil
1 spring onion (scallion), cut into short
   sections
1 tsp salt
$^1/_2$ tsp sugar
1 tbsp light soy sauce
1 tsp chilli bean sauce or freshly minced
   chilli
1 tsp rice wine or dry sherry
a few drops of sesame oil

1 Immerse the pork in a pot of boiling water to cover. Return to the boil and skim the surface. Reduce the heat, cover and simmer for 15-20 minutes. Turn off the heat and leave the pork in the water to cool for at least 2-3 hours.

2 Remove the pork from the water and drain well. Trim off any excess fat, then cut into small, thin slices. Cut the green and red (bell) peppers into pieces about the same size as the pork and the sliced bamboo shoots.

3 Heat the oil in a preheated wok and add the vegetables together with the spring onion (scallion). Stir-fry for about 1 minute.

4 Add the pork, followed by the salt, sugar, soy sauce, chilli bean sauce and wine. Blend well, continue stirring for another minute, then sprinkle with sesame oil and serve.

PREPARING THE MEAT

For ease of handling, buy a boned piece of meat, and roll into a compact shape. Tie securely with string before placing in the boiling water.

STEP 1

STEP 2

STEP 3

STEP 4

CRISPY SHREDDED BEEF

A very popular Szechuan dish served in most Chinese restaurants all over the world.

SERVES 4

300-350 g/10-12 oz beef steak (such as
   topside or rump)
2 eggs
¼ tsp salt
4-5 tbsp plain flour
vegetable oil for deep-frying
2 medium carrots, finely shredded
2 spring onions (scallions), thinly shredded
1 garlic clove, finely chopped
2-3 small fresh green or red chillies, seeded
   and thinly shredded
4 tbsp sugar
3 tbsp rice vinegar
1 tbsp light soy sauce
2-3 tbsp Chinese Stock (see page 76) or
   water
1 tsp cornflour (cornstarch) paste (see
   page 77)

1 Cut the steak across the grain into thin strips. Beat the eggs in a bowl with the salt and flour, adding a little water if necessary. Add the beef strips and mix well until coated with the batter.

2 Heat the oil in a preheated wok until smoking. Add the beef strips and deep-fry for 4-5 minutes, stirring to separate the shreds. Remove with a slotted spoon and drain on paper towels.

3 Add the carrots to the wok and deep-fry for about 1-1½ minutes, then remove with a slotted spoon and drain on paper towels.

4 Pour off the excess oil, leaving about 1 tablespoon in the wok. Add the spring onions (scallions), garlic, chillies and carrots, stir-fry for about 1 minute, then add the sugar, vinegar, soy sauce and stock or water, blend well and bring to the boil.

5 Stir in the cornflour (cornstarch) paste and simmer for a few minutes to thicken the sauce. Return the beef to the wok and stir until the shreds of meat are well coated with the sauce. Serve hot.

TEXTURES

This dish is typical of the chewy-textured food that is so popular in Szechuan. Unlike dishes in Eastern China many Szechuan dishes are fried with only the minimum of sauce to convey the seasonings: the sauce itself is not an important element in the dish as in Canton.

BEEF & CHILLI BLACK BEAN SAUCE

It is not necessary to use the expensive cuts of beef steak for this recipe: the meat will be tender as it is cut into small thin slices and marinated.

STEP 1

SERVES 4

250-300 g/8-10 oz beef steak (such as rump)
1 small onion
1 small green (bell) pepper, cored and seeded
about 300 ml/¹/₂ pint/ 1¹/₄ cups vegetable oil
1 spring onion (scallion), cut into short sections
a few small slices of ginger root
1-2 small green or red chillies, seeded and sliced
2 tbsp crushed black bean sauce

MARINADE:
¹/₂ tsp bicarbonate of soda or baking powder
¹/₂ tsp sugar
1 tbsp light soy sauce
2 tsp rice wine or dry sherry
2 tsp cornflour (cornstarch) paste (see page 77)
2 tsp sesame oil

1 Cut the beef into small thin strips. Mix together the marinade ingredients in a shallow dish, add the beef strips, turn to coat and leave to marinate for at least 2-3 hours – the longer the better.

2 Cut the onion and green (bell) pepper into small cubes.

3 Heat the oil in a pre-heated wok. Add the beef strips and stir-fry for about 1 minute, or until the colour changes. Remove with a slotted spoon and drain on paper towels. Keep warm.

4 Pour off the excess oil, leaving about 1 tablespoon in the wok. Add the spring onion (scallion), ginger, chillies, onion and green (bell) pepper and stir-fry for about 1 minute. Add the black bean sauce, stir until smooth then return the beef strips to the wok. Blend well and stir-fry for another minute. Serve hot.

STEP 1

STEP 2

STEP 3

MARINADES

Do make sure that you marinade the beef for the time specified – it will then be wonderfully soft and tender.

STEP 4

CHAPTER FIVE

Vegetables, Rice & Noodles

With the fertile soil and warm, humid climate Szechuan is one of
the most prosperous regions of China, and crops can be grown
almost all year round. Fruit, vegetables and cereal crops
grow in abundance, as well as mushrooms and fungi.
Pickling, drying and salting techniques are used extensively
to help preserve this abundance of food – partly because
the humid climate makes it difficult
to keep food fresh.

As with other dishes, these tend to be highly spiced, and are usually
on the hot side. "Fish-flavoured", as in the aubergine (eggplant)
dish on page 65, sounds strange, but is a popular way of describing
dishes cooked with a variety of spices and flavourings –
it has nothing to do with fish,
and tastes delicious!

Opposite: *Rice plants hanging
up to dry on bamboo racks. Rice
is a staple crop in China and the
fertile soil of Szechuan produces
vast quantities of it.*

STEP 1

STEP 2

STEP 3

STEP 4

MA-PO TOFU

Ma-Po was the wife of a Szechuan chef who created this popular dish in the middle of the 19th century. The beef can be replaced by Chinese dried mushrooms to make a vegetarian meal.

SERVES 4

3 cakes tofu (bean curd)
3 tbsp vegetable oil
125g/4 oz coarsely minced (ground) beef
½ tsp finely chopped garlic
1 leek, cut into short sections
½ tsp salt
1 tbsp black bean sauce
1 tbsp light soy sauce
1 tsp chilli bean sauce
3-4 tbsp Chinese Stock (see page 76) or water
2 tsp cornflour (cornstarch) paste (see page 77)
a few drops of sesame oil
black pepper
finely chopped spring onions (scallions), to garnish

1 Cut the tofu into 1 cm/½ in cubes, handling it carefully. Bring some water to the boil in a small pan or a wok, add the tofu and blanch for 2-3 minutes to harden. Remove and drain well.

2 Heat the oil in a preheated wok. Add the minced (ground) beef and garlic and stir-fry for about 1 minute, or until the colour of the beef changes. Add the chopped leek, salt and sauces and blend well.

3 Add the stock or water followed by the tofu. Bring to the boil and braise gently for 2-3 minutes.

4 Add the cornflour (cornstarch) paste, and stir until the sauce has thickened. Sprinkle with sesame oil and black pepper and garnish with spring onions (scallions). Serve hot.

TOFU (BEAN CURD)

Tofu has been an important element in Chinese cooking for more than 1000 years. It is made of yellow soya beans, which are soaked, ground and mixed with water. Tofu is highly nutritious, being rich in protein, and has a very bland taste. Solid cakes of tofu can be cut up with a sharp knife. Cook carefully as too much stirring can cause it to disintegrate.

60

STEP 1a

STEP 1b

STEP 3

STEP 4

BRAISED TOFU HOME STYLE

The pork used in the recipe can be replaced by chicken or prawns (shrimps), or it can be omitted altogether.

SERVES 4

3 cakes tofu (bean curd)
125 g/4 oz boneless pork (or any other type
of meat)
1 leek
1-2 spring onions (scallions), cut into short
sections
a few small dried whole chillies, soaked
vegetable oil, for deep-frying
2 tbsp crushed yellow bean sauce
1 tbsp light soy sauce
2 tsp rice wine or dry sherry
a few drops of sesame oil

1 Split each cake of tofu into 3 slices crosswise, then cut each slice diagonally into 2 triangles.

2 Cut the pork into small thin slices or shreds; cut the leek into thin strips. Drain the chillies, remove the seeds using the tip of a knife, then cut into small shreds.

3 Heat the oil in a preheated wok until smoking, then deep-fry the tofu triangles for 2-3 minutes, or until golden brown all over. Remove with a slotted spoon and drain on paper towels.

4 Pour off the hot oil, leaving about 1 tablespoon in the wok. Add the pork

strips, spring onions (scallions) and chillies and stir-fry for about 1 minute or until the pork changes colour.

5 Add the leek, tofu, yellow bean sauce, soy sauce and wine and braise for 2-3 minutes, stirring very gently to blend everything well. Finally sprinkle on the sesame oil and serve.

BRAISED TOFU

Tofu is sold in 2 forms: as firm cakes, or as a thickish junket, known as silken tofu. It is the solid kind that is used for braising and stir-frying. Silken tofu is usually added to soups or sauces. It is also possible to buy dried tofu and smoked tofu in specialist oriental stores. It is acceptable to store tofu for a few days if it is submerged in water in an air-tight container, then placed in the refrigerator.

FISH AUBERGINE (EGGPLANT)

*Like Fish-flavoured Shredded Pork (page 50), there is no fish involved in
this dish, and the meat can be omitted without affecting the flavour.*

STEP 1

SERVES 4

500 g/1 lb aubergine (eggplant)
vegetable oil, for deep-frying
1 garlic clove, finely chopped
¹/₂ tsp finely chopped ginger root
2 spring onions (scallions), finely chopped,
  with the white and green parts separated
125 g/4 oz pork, thinly shredded (optional)
1 tbsp light soy sauce
2 tsp rice wine or dry sherry
1 tbsp chilli bean sauce
¹/₂ tsp salt
¹/₂ tsp sugar
1 tbsp rice vinegar
2 tsp cornflour (cornstarch) paste (see
  page 77)
a few drops of sesame oil

1 Cut the aubergine (eggplant) into
rounds and then into thin strips
about the size of potato chips – the skin
can either be peeled or left on.

2 Heat the oil in a preheated wok
until smoking. Add the aubergine
(eggplant) chips and deep-fry for about 3-
4 minutes, or until soft. Remove and
drain on paper towels.

3 Pour off the hot oil, leaving about 1
tablespoon in the wok. Add the

garlic, ginger and the white parts of the
spring onions (scallions), followed by the
pork (if using). Stir-fry for about 1
minute or until the colour of the meat
changes, then add the soy sauce, wine
and chilli bean sauce, blending them in
well.

4 Return the aubergine (eggplant)
chips to the wok together with the
salt, sugar and vinegar. Continue stirring
for another minute or so, then add the
cornflour (cornstarch) paste and stir
until the sauce has thickened.

5 Add the green parts of the spring
onions (scallions) to the wok and
sprinkle on the sesame oil. Serve hot.

STEP 2

STEP 3

FISH-FLAVOURED DISHES

These multiple flavoured dishes, using
garlic, chilli sauce, vinegar, sugar and soy
sauce all together, are always described
as "fish-flavoured" although there is no
fish in the recipe. These dishes are only
found in Szechuan.

STEP 4

STEP 1

STEP 2

STEP 3

STEP 4

STIR-FRIED SEASONAL VEGETABLES

When selecting different fresh vegetables for this dish, bear in mind that there should always be a contrast in colour as well as texture.

SERVES 4

1 medium red (bell) pepper, cored and seeded
125g/4 oz courgettes (zucchini)
125g/4 oz cauliflower
125g/4 oz French beans
3tbsp vegetable oil
a few small slices ginger root
$\frac{1}{2}$ tsp salt
$\frac{1}{2}$ tsp sugar
Chinese Stock (see page 76) or water
1 tbsp light soy sauce
a few drops of sesame oil (optional)

1 Cut the red (bell) pepper into small squares. Thinly slice the courgettes (zucchini). Trim the cauliflower and divide into small florets, discarding any thick stems. Make sure the vegetables are cut into roughly similar shapes and sizes to ensure even cooking.

2 Top and tail the French beans, then cut them in half.

3 Heat the oil in a pre-heated wok, add the vegetables and stir-fry with the ginger for about 2 minutes.

4 Add the salt and sugar to the wok, and continue to stir-fry for 1-2 minutes, adding a little Chinese stock

or water if the vegetables appear to be too dry. Do not add liquid unless it seems necessary.

5 Add the light soy sauce and sesame oil (if using) blend well to lightly coat the vegetables and serve immediately.

VEGETABLES

Almost any vegetables could be used in this dish: other good choices would be mangetout (snow peas), broccoli florets, carrots, baby corn cobs, green peas, Chinese cabbage and young spinach leaves. Either white or black (oyster) mushrooms can also be used to give a greater diversity of textures. Make sure there is a good variety of colour, and always include several crisp vegetables such as carrots or mangetout (snow peas).

STEP 1

STEP 2

STEP 3

STEP 4

BRAISED CHINESE LEAVES

White cabbage can be used instead of the Chinese leaves for this dish.

SERVES 4

500 g / 1 lb Chinese leaves or white cabbage
3 tbsp vegetable oil
$^1/_2$ tsp Szechuan red peppercorns
5-6 small dried red chillies, seeded and
    chopped
$^1/_2$ tsp salt
1 tbsp sugar
1 tbsp light soy sauce
1 tbsp rice vinegar
a few drops of sesame oil (optional)

1 Shred the Chinese leaves or cabbage crosswise into thin pieces. (If Chinese leaves are unavailable, the best alternative to use in this recipe is a firm-packed white cabbage, not the dark green type of cabbage. Cut out the thick core of the cabbage with a sharp knife before shredding.)

2 Heat the oil in a pre-heated wok, add the Szechuan red peppercorns and dried red chillies and stir for a few seconds.

3 Add the Chinese leaves or shredded cabbage to the peppercorns and chillies, stir-fry for about 1 minute, then add salt and continue stirring for another minute.

4 Add the sugar, soy sauce and vinegar, blend well and braise for one more minute. Finally sprinkle on the sesame oil, if using. Serve hot or cold.

PEPPERCORNS

It is important to use the correct type of peppercorns in preparing this dish. Szechuan red peppercorns are also known as farchiew. They are not true peppers, but reddish brown dry berries with a pungent, aromatic odour which distinguishes them from the hotter black peppercorns. Roast them briefly in the oven or sauté them in a dry frying pan (skillet). Grind the peppercorns in a blender and store in a jar until needed.

STEP 2

STEP 3

STEP 4

CHICKEN OR PORK CHOW MEIN

*This is a basic recipe – the meat and/or vegetables can be
varied as much as you like.*

SERVES 4

250 g/8 oz egg noodles
4-5 tbsp vegetable oil
125g/4 oz French beans
250 g/8 oz chicken breast meat, or pork
  fillet, cooked
2 tbsp light soy sauce
1 tsp salt
½ tsp sugar
1 tbsp Chinese rice wine or dry sherry
2 spring onions (scallions), finely shredded
a few drops of sesame oil
chilli sauce, to serve (optional)

1 Cook the noodles in boiling water
according to the instructions on
the packet, then drain and rinse under
cold water. Drain again then toss with 1
tablespoon of the oil.

2 Slice the meat into thin shreds and
top and tail the beans.

3 Heat 3 tablespoons of oil in a
preheated wok until hot, add the
noodles and stir-fry for 2-3 minutes with
1 tablespoon soy sauce, then remove to a
serving dish. Keep warm.

4 Heat the remaining oil and stir-fry
the beans and meat for about 2

minutes. Add the salt, sugar, wine, the
remaining soy sauce and about half the
spring onions (scallions) to the wok.

5 Blend the meat mixture well and
add a little stock if necessary, then
pour on top of the noodles, and sprinkle
with sesame oil and the remaining spring
onions (scallions). Serve hot or cold with
or without chilli sauce.

CHOW MEIN

Chow Mein literally means "stir-fried
noodles" and is highly popular in the West
as well as in China. Almost any ingredient
can be added, such as fish, meat, poultry
or vegetables. It is very popular for lunch
and makes a tasty salad served cold.

STEP 2

STEP 3

STEP 4

STEP 5

NOODLES IN SOUP

Noodles in soup (tang mein) are far more popular than fried noodles (chow mein) in China. You can use different ingredients for the dressing according to taste.

SERVES 4

250 g/8 oz chicken fillet, pork fillet, or any
other ready-cooked meat
3-4 Chinese dried mushrooms, soaked
125 g/4 oz canned sliced bamboo shoots,
rinsed and drained
125 g/4 oz spinach leaves, lettuce hearts, or
Chinese leaves, shredded
2 spring onions (scallions), finely shredded
250 g/8 oz egg noodles
about 600 ml/1pint/2¹/₂ cups Chinese Stock
(see page 76)
2 tbsp light soy sauce
2 tbsp vegetable oil
1 tsp salt
¹/₂ tsp sugar
2 tsp Chinese rice wine or dry sherry
a few drops of sesame oil
1 tsp red chilli oil (optional)

1 Cut the meat into thin shreds. Squeeze dry the soaked mushrooms and discard the hard stalk.

2 Thinly shred the mushrooms, bamboo shoots, spinach leaves and spring onions (scallions).

3 Cook the noodles in boiling water according to the instructions on the packet, then drain and rinse under cold water. Place in a bowl. Bring the stock to a boil, add about 1 tablespoon soy sauce and pour over the noodles. Keep warm.

4 Heat the oil in a pre-heated wok, add about half of the spring onions (scallions), the meat and the vegetables (mushrooms, bamboo shoots and greens). Stir-fry for about 2-3 minutes. Add all the seasonings and blend well.

5 Pour the mixture in the wok over the noodles, garnish with the remaining spring onions (scallions) and serve immediately.

NOODLE SOUP

Noodle soup is wonderfully satisfying and is ideal to serve on cold winter days.

EGG FRIED RICE

*The rice used for frying should not be too soft. Ideally, the rice should
have been slightly under-cooked and left to cool before frying.*

SERVES 4

3 eggs
1 tsp salt
2 spring onions (scallions), finely chopped
2-3 tbsp vegetable oil
*500 g/ 1 lb/ 3 cups cooked rice, well drained
and cooled (see note in step 3)*
125 g/ 4 oz cooked peas

1 Lightly beat the eggs with a pinch
of salt and 1 tablespoon of the
spring onions (scallions).

2 Heat the oil in a preheated wok,
add the eggs and stir until lightly
scrambled. (The eggs should only be
cooked until they start to set, so they are
still moist.)

3 Add the rice and stir to make sure
that each grain of rice is separated.
Note: the cooked rice should be cool,
preferably cold, so that much of the
moisture has evaporated. This ensures
that the oil will coat the grains of rice and
prevent them sticking. Store the cooked
rice in the refrigerator until ready to
cook. Make sure the oil is really hot
before adding the rice, to avoid the rice
being saturated with oil otherwise it will
be heavy and greasy.

4 Add the remaining salt, spring
onions (scallions) and peas. Blend
well and serve hot or cold.

PERFECT FRIED RICE

Use rice with a fairly firm texture. Ideally,
the raw rice should be soaked in water for
a short time before cooking. The two main
varieties of rice available are long-grain
and short-grain. While it used to be
necessary to wash rice, processing now
makes this unnecessary. Short-grain
Oriental rice can be substituted for long-
grain.

Fried rice lends itself to many
variations. You may choose to add other
vegetables as well as the spring onions
(scallions), if desired, as well as prawns
(shrimp), ham or chicken.

STEP 1

STEP 2

STEP 3

STEP 4

SZECHUAN COOKING

CHINESE STOCK

This basic stock is used not only as the basis for soup-making, but also for general use in Chinese cooking.

MAKES 2.5 L/4 PINTS/
10 CUPS

750 g/1½ lb chicken pieces
750 g/1½ lb pork spare ribs
3.75 litres /6 pints/15 cups cold
    water
3-4 pieces ginger root, crushed
3-4 spring onions (scallions),
    each tied into a knot
3-4 tbsp Chinese rice wine or dry
    sherry

1. Trim off excess fat from the chicken and spare ribs; chop them into large pieces.

2. Place the chicken and pork in a large pan with water; add the ginger and spring onion (scallion) knots.

3. Bring to the boil, and skim off the scum. Reduce heat and simmer uncovered for at least 2-3 hours.

4. Strain the stock, discarding the chicken, pork, ginger and spring onions (scallions); add the wine and return to the boil, simmer for 2-3 minutes.

Refrigerate the stock when cool, it will keep up to 4-5 days. Alternatively, it can be frozen in small containers and be defrosted as required.

Szechuan, the largest single province in China, lies in a great basin ringed with mountains. Its principal connection eastwards is through spectacular gorges cut by the Yangtse River – until recently, in fact, the Yangtse was its only means of communication with the outside world. With its fertile soil and warm, humid climate crops can be grown almost all the year round, and it has always been one of the most prosperous regions of China. Fruit and vegetables grow in abundance, as well as edible mushrooms and fungi. Spices grow in abundance here too, particularly chillis and the famous Szechuan peppercorns.

Szechuan food is noted for being hot, spicy and strongly flavoured. Chillis are used in large quantities – usually unseeded – as well as pungent flavoured vegetables such as garlic, onions and spring onions. The inhabitants also enjoy the aromatic, nutty flavour of peanuts, sesame seeds, cashews, walnuts and pine nuts, which are often found incorporated into dishes; aromatic ground rice and sesame seeds are often used to coat meat which is to be deep-fried or stir-fried, while sesame paste is often the principal ingredient in sauces.

The region is also noted for its food preservation techniques, which include salting, drying, smoking and pickling, probably because the humid climate makes it difficult to keep food fresh.

Beef appears more often on the menu here than in the south. A favourite way of cooking it is by stir-frying, often until it is quite dry, giving it the characteristic dry "chewy" texture. Steaming is also popular, and here the meat is usually first coated with ground rice, producing a rich, thick gravy.

Yunnan, in the deep south west, is even more remote than Szechuan. Being so mountainous and secluded, it developed over the years a highly distinctive cuisine of its own. The best known product of Yunnan is its ham, which many Chinese consider the best in the world. It is also noted for its game, such as rabbit and venison, and it is here that such exotic items as bear's paws, snails, armadillo, slugs and snakes can appear on the menu!

EQUIPMENT AND UTENSILS

There are only a few basic implements in the Chinese batterie de cuisine that are considered essential in order to achieve the best results. Equivalent equipment is always available in a Western kitchen, but Chinese cooking utensils are of an ancient design, usually made of inexpensive materials; they have been in continuous use for several thousand of years and do serve a special function. Their more sophisticated and much more expensive Western counterparts prove rather inadequate in contrast.

Chinese cleaver An all-purpose cook's knife that is used for slicing, shredding, peeling, crushing and chopping. Different sizes and weights are available.

Wok The round-bottomed iron wok conducts and retains heat evenly, and because of its shape, the ingredients always return to the centre, where the heat is most intense, however vigorously you stir. The wok is also ideal for deep-frying – its conical shape requires far less oil than the flat-bottomed deep-fryer, and has more depth (which means more heat) and more cooking surface (which means more food can be cooked at one go). Besides being a frying-pan, a wok is also used for braising, steaming, boiling and poaching etc – in other words, the whole spectrum of Chinese cooking methods can be executed in one single utensil.

Ladle and spatula Some wok sets usually consist of a pair of stirrers in the form of a ladle and spatula. Of the two, the flat ladle or scooper (as it is sometimes called) is more versatile. It is used by the Chinese cook for adding ingredients and seasonings to the wok besides being a stirring implement.

Strainers There are two basic types of strainers – one is made of copper or steel wire with long bamboo handles, the other of perforated metal (iron or stainless steel). Several different sizes are available.

Steamers The traditional Chinese steamer is made of bamboo and they can be stacked on top of each other. The modern version is made of aluminum. Of course, the wok can be used on its own as a steamer with a rack or trivet and the dome-shaped wok lid.

Chopsticks Does Chinese food taste any better when eaten with chopsticks? This is not merely an aesthetic question, but also a practical point, partly because all Chinese food is prepared in such a way that it is easily picked up by chopsticks.

Learning to use chopsticks is quite simple and easy – place one chopstick in the hollow between thumb and index finger and rest its lower end below the first joint of the third finger. This chopstick remains stationary. Hold the other chopstick between the tips of the index and middle finger, steady its upper half against the base of the index finger, and use the tip of the thumb to keep it in place. To pick up food, move the upper chopstick with index and middle fingers.

GLOSSARY OF INGREDIENTS USED IN CHINESE COOKING

Baby sweetcorn Baby corn cobs have a wonderfully sweet fragrance and flavour, and an irresistible texture. They are available both fresh and canned.

Bamboo shoots Available in cans only. Once opened, the contents may be kept in fresh water in a covered jar for up to a week in the refrigerator.

Bean-sprouts Fresh bean-sprouts, from mung or soya beans, are widely available from Oriental stores and supermarkets. They can be kept in the refrigerator for two to three days.

Black bean sauce Sold in jars or cans. Salted beans are crushed and mixed with flour and spices (such as ginger, garlic or

CORNFLOUR (CORNSTARCH) PASTE

Cornflour (cornstarch) paste is made by mixing 1 part cornflour (cornstarch) with about 1.5 parts of cold water. Stir until smooth. The paste is used to thicken sauces.

PRAWNS (SHRIMP) WITH DIP SAUCE

300 g (10oz) raw prawns (shrimp), defrosted if frozen
1 tsp salt
1 litre/2 pints/4 cups water
2 spring onions (scallions), shredded
2-3 slices ginger root, shredded
2 green or red chillies, seeded and finely shredded
1 tbsp vegetable oil
2 tbsp light soy sauce
1 tbsp red rice vinegar
1 tsp sesame oil

1. Poach the prawns (shrimp) in boiling, salted water for 1 minute, then turn off the heat. Leave to stand for 1 minute then remove with a slotted spoon and drain.

2. Place the spring onions (scallions), ginger and chillies in a small heatproof bowl. Heat the oil until hot and pour into the bowl. Add the soy sauce, vinegar and sesame oil.

3. Shell the prawns (shrimp), leaving the tails, and arrange on a serving dish. Serve with the dip sauce.

PLAIN RICE

Use long-grain or patna rice, or better still, try fragrant Thai rice.

SERVES 4
250 g/8 oz long-grain rice
about 200 ml/7 fl oz cold water
pinch of salt
½ tsp oil (optional)

1. Wash and rinse the rice just once. Place the rice in a saucepan and add enough water so that there is no more than 2 cm/¾ in of water above the surface of the rice.

2. Bring to the boil, add salt and oil (if using), and stir to prevent the rice sticking to the bottom of the pan.

3. Reduce the heat to very, very low, cover and cook for 15-20 minutes.

4. Remove from the heat and let stand, covered, for 10 minutes or so. Fluff up the rice with a fork or spoon before serving.

chilli etc) to make a thickish paste. Once opened, keep in the refrigerator.

Chilli bean sauce Fermented bean paste mixed with hot chilli and other seasonings. Sold in jars, some sauces are quite mild, but others are very hot. You will have to try out the various brands to see which one is to your taste.

Chilli sauce Very hot sauce made from chillis, vinegar, sugar and salt. Usually sold in bottles and should be used sparingly in cooking or as a dip. Tabasco sauce can be a substitute.

Chinese leaves Also known as Chinese cabbage, there are two widely available varieties in supermarkets and greengrocers. The most commonly seen one is a pale green colour and has a tightly wrapped, elongated head – about two-thirds of the cabbage is stem, which has a crunchy texture. The other variety has a shorter, fatter head with curlier, pale yellow or green leaves, also with white stems.

Coriander Fresh coriander leaves, also known as Chinese parsley or cilantro, are widely used in Chinese cooking as a garnish.

Dried Chinese mushrooms (Shiitake) Highly fragrant dried mushrooms which add a special flavour to Chinese dishes. There are many different varieties, but Shiitake are the best. They are not cheap, but a small amount will go a long way, and they will keep indefinitely in an airtight jar. Soak them in warm water for

20-30 minutes (or in cold water for several hours), squeeze dry and discard the hard stalks before use.

Egg noodles There are many varieties of noodles in China, ranging from flat, broad ribbons to long narrow strands. Both dried and fresh noodles are available.

Five-spice powder A mixture of star anise, fennel seeds, cloves, cinnamon bark and Szechuan pepper. It is very pungent, so should be used sparingly. It will keep in an airtight container indefinitely.

Ginger root Fresh ginger root, sold by weight, should be peeled then sliced, finely chopped or shredded before use. It will keep for weeks in a dry, cool place. Dried ginger powder is no substitute.

Hoi-sin sauce Also known as barbecue sauce, this is made from soy beans, sugar, flour, vinegar, salt, garlic, chilli and sesame seed oil. Sold in cans or jars, it will keep in the refrigerator for several months.

Oyster sauce A thickish soy-based sauce used as a flavouring in Cantonese cooking. Sold in bottles, it will keep in the refrigerator for months.

Plum sauce Plum sauce has a unique, fruity flavour – a sweet and sour sauce with a difference.

Rice vinegar There are two basic types of rice vinegar. Red vinegar is made from fermented rice and has a distinctive dark colour and depth of flavour. White vinegar is stronger in flavour as it is distilled from rice wine.

Rice wine Chinese rice wine, made from glutinous rice, is also known as "Yellow wine" (Huang jiu or chiew in Chinese), because of its golden amber colour. The best variety is called Shao Hsing or Shaoxing from south-east China. A good dry or medium sherry can be an acceptable substitute.

Sesame oil This aromatic oil is sold in bottles and widely used as a finishing touch, added to dishes just before serving. The refined yellow sesame oil sold in middle-eastern stores is not so aromatic, has less flavour and therefore is not a very satisfactory substitute for the real thing.

Soy sauce Sold in bottles or cans, this popular Chinese sauce is used both for cooking and at the table. Light soy sauce has more flavour than the sweeter dark soy sauce, which gives the food a rich, reddish colour.

Straw mushrooms Grown on beds of rice straw, hence the name, straw mushrooms have a pleasant slippery texture, and a subtle taste. Canned straw mushrooms should be rinsed and drained after opening.

Szechuan peppercorns Also known as farchiew, these are wild reddish-brown peppercorns from Szechuan. More aromatic but less hot than either white or black peppercorns, they do give a quite unique flavour to the food.

Szechuan preserved vegetables The pickled mustard root is very hot and salty. Sold in cans. Once opened, it should be stored in a tightly sealed jar in the refrigerator.

Tofu (bean curd) This custard-like preparation of puréed and pressed soya beans is exceptionally high in protein. It is usually sold in cakes about 7.5 cm/3 in square and 2.5 cm/1 in thick in Oriental and health-food stores. Will keep for a few days if submerged in water in a container and placed in the refrigerator.

Water chestnuts The roots of the plant *Heleocharis tuberosa*. Also known as horse's hooves in China on account of their appearance before the skin is peeled off. They are available fresh or in cans. Canned water chestnuts do not have the texture, and even less the flavour, of fresh ones. Will keep for about a month in the refrigerator in a covered jar, changing the water every two or three days.

Wood ears Also known as cloud ears, this is a dried black fungus. Sold in plastic bags in Oriental stores, it should be soaked in cold or warm water for 20 minutes, then rinsed in fresh water before use. It has a crunchy texture and a mild but subtle flavour.

Yellow bean sauce A thick paste made from salted, fermented yellow soya beans, crushed with flour and sugar. It is sold in cans or jars.

CHINESE FRUIT SALAD

The Chinese do not usually have desserts to finish off a meal, except at banquets and special occasions. Sweet dishes are usually served in between main meals as snacks, but fruit is refreshing at the end of a big meal.

250 g/8 oz rock candy or crystal sugar
600 ml/1 pint boiling water
1 large honeydew melon
4-5 different fruits, such as pineapple, grapes, banana, mango, lychees or kiwi fruit

1. Dissolve the rock candy in the boiling water, then leave to cool.

2. Slice 2.5 cm/1 in off the top of the melon and scoop out the flesh, discarding the seeds. Cut the flesh into small chunks. Prepare the other fruits and cut into small chunks.

3. Fill the melon shell with the fruits and the syrup. Cover with clingfilm and chill for at least 2 hours. Serve on a bed of crushed ice.

INDEX